Brittany Gilmore

Dood and the First Day of School

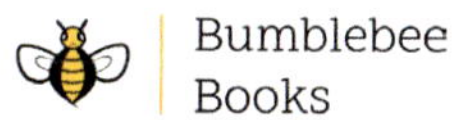

Bumblebee Books is an imprint of
Olympia Publishers.

First Published in 2023

Bumblebee Books
Tallis House
2 Tallis Street
London
EC4Y 0AB
Printed in Great Britain

Dedication

For my loves, Jack & Finnie.

For Presley, Cash, & Navy.

And for all of the children who read this story.

I hope you always know how truly special

and unique you are!

Dood was the happiest pup in the whole wide world. He loved his days of going to the park, playing frisbee with Mom and Dad, napping, and eating his favorite foods. Dood didn't have a single worry.

Then one day Mom and Dad told Dood he would be going to a place called school.

They said he would meet new friends, learn new tricks, and have so much fun.

Dood felt excited and also a little bit scared. He didn't like change. He wanted to stay home and continue to do all of the things he loved.

Nevertheless, Dood put on his favorite bandana, packed his favorite lunch, and decided to be brave.

Dood loved his new teacher, Mrs. Puppins. He learned new tricks that he couldn't wait to show Mom and Dad. He even met a new, playful friend named Hogan.

Then at lunch time someone made fun of the way Dood's favorite lunch smelt. The other pups laughed. Dood threw it away and went hungry.

At play time, that same someone teased Dood about his "big, floppy ears". The other pups laughed some more.

Dood couldn't help but notice that nobody else had ears like his. He hid for the rest of play time.

When Dood's mom and dad came to pick him up, they noticed he wasn't the same pup they dropped off. They asked him what was wrong.

Dood did not want to worry his parents so he told them he had a great day.

He felt bad for lying to them.

Dood told himself he was never returning to that place called school. The next morning Dood pretended to be sick, and Mom and Dad let him stay home to rest.

At first, he felt happy...

But then he felt sad that he wouldn't get to see Hogan and Mrs. Puppins or learn new tricks.

Dood couldn't stop thinking about his
big, floppy ears.

"Were they really that bad?" Dood
wondered as he cried in his bed.

Mom came in and noticed Dood crying. She asked him what was wrong. Dood told her that he hated his once favorite meal and especially hated his big, floppy ears!

Mom kissed Dood's head and wondered where all of this was coming from. She asked if it had to do with school and Dood froze.

He broke down and told Mom everything through a lot of puppy tears. He felt relieved after telling Mom the truth about the bad parts of his first day.

Mom helped Dood to realize that everyone likes and eats different foods. And that every pup has something that makes them special and unique. Afterall, nobody has ears quite like Doods.

Mom asked Dood about the good parts of his first day. Dood beamed with pride as he showed Mom all the new tricks he learned. He told her about the wonderful Mrs. Puppins and the playful Hogan.

He chose to remember and retell the good parts and he felt a whole lot better.

Mom asked Dood if he
was ready to face school
tomorrow.
He didn't know if he could do it.

Then he remembered all the things he
and Mom talked about. He decided he
wanted to try again, one more time. He
knew the longer he waited the harder it
would be.

The next morning Dood felt very nervous. His heart raced, his paws were sweating, and his tummy was full of butterflies. He took a deep breath and said to himself, "I can do this!"

He packed his favorite lunch, put on his lucky bandana, and decided to be brave once more.

And he was glad he did! Mrs. Puppins was happy to see him and he learned even more cool, new tricks.

Hogan and Dood shared their lunches together and found they enjoyed the same things.

While playing frisbee Dood was by far the highest jumper,
his ears launching him towards the sky!

All the other pups were talking about how fast Dood was and how his ears seemed to make him fly.

Dood noticed that same someone off by themselves, looking sad. He asked him to play, knowing what it felt like to be alone.

The pup smiled and joined Dood and the others. When he saw Dood's high jumps he told Dood he wished he had ears just like his.

Dood told him that every pup has something that makes them special and unique.

When Mom and Dad came to pick Dood up, they found a smiling, confident pup.

Dood couldn't wait to tell them all about his day
and show off his cool, new tricks.

Building Social/Emotional Awareness

1. What happened at school that made Dood not want to go back?
2. What helped Dood to feel better and ready to return to school?
3. What happened in Dood's body when he felt nervous?
4. How did Dood's ears end up helping him?
5. What makes you feel special and unique?

About the Author

Brittany Gilmore is a Licensed Marriage and Family Therapist who works with children, adolescents, and their families to support in the development of healthy coping, relational dynamics, decision-making, self-esteem, and more. Her passion is providing a safe space for others to explore, process, and reflect in order to experience positive change, growth, and overall well-being. Reading and writing have also been a passion of hers since childhood and Dood and the First Day of School is the start of her dream in engaging a wider audience in a fun, relatable, and impactful way through the eyes of her real-life doodle dog, Finnegan.

Acknowledgements

Thank you to my husband, Jarad, for your love, confidence, encouragement, and support in all things, including writing this book. Thank you to my mother, sister, and dear friends for your unwavering love and support in all that I do. And thank you to all of the children and families that have allowed me to be a part of your journey.